LOVE SONG

John Kolvenbach
LOVE SONG

OBERON BOOKS
LONDON

First published in 2006 by Oberon Books Ltd
521 Caledonian Road, London N7 9RH
Tel: 020 7607 3637 / Fax: 020 7607 3629
e-mail: info@oberonbooks.com
www.oberonbooks.com

A catalogue record for this book is available from the British Library.

Cover design by aka / Cover photographs by Eric Richmond

ISBN: 1 84002 715 0 / 978-1-84002-715-0

for my sisters

Characters

BEANE

JOAN

HARRY

MOLLY

WAITER

Square brackets indicate a change in tone.
Parentheses contain stage directions.

Love Song received its world premiere in March 2006, produced by Steppenwolf Theatre Company, Chicago, with the following company:

BEANE, Ian Barford
JOAN, Molly Regan
HARRY / WAITER, Francis Guinan
MOLLY, Mariann Mayberry

Directed by Austin Pendleton
Scenic design by Brian Sidney Bembridge
Costume design by Rachel Anne Healy
Lighting design by Michelle Habeck
Sound design by Andre Pluess & Ben Sussman
Casting by Erica Daniels

Love Song received its European premiere in the West End of London at the New Ambassadors Theatre on 25 November 2006, produced by Sonia Friedman Productions, Robert G Bartner and Boyett Ostar Productions, with the following company:

BEANE, Cillian Murphy
JOAN, Kristen Johnston
HARRY, Michael McKean
MOLLY, Neve Campbell
WAITER, James Scales

Directed by John Crowley
Set design by Scott Pask
Costume design by Jack Galloway
Lighting design by Howard Harrison
Sound design by Paul Arditti
Casting by Jim Carnahan

SCENE ONE

BEANE's apartment.

In a small, spare, studio apartment, BEANE sits at a wooden table. He wears an overcoat. The apartment is cold. The walls, once white, are gray and stained. They are unadorned.

The room is lit by a single source. A standing lamp.

Pause. The lamp dims. BEANE notes the change. The lamp dims further. Pause.

BEANE crosses to the lamp which stands next to a tattered armchair.

BEANE nudges the lamp. It dims further, as if in hostile response.

He crosses to the wooden table. He sits.

The walls and ceiling converge on BEANE's head.

They move a couple of feet, perhaps. The movement is not sudden. It's not that he will be crushed. Rather, he might, over a couple of days, be suffocated.

BEANE notes the movement of the walls and of the ceiling. He is uncomfortable, but he is not surprised. He accepts his shrinking, darkening world with a weary sigh.

The light dims further. The walls move in another foot or so.

BEANE sits at a wooden table in his overcoat.

Lights.

SCENE TWO

JOAN and HARRY's apartment.

A tasteful two-bedroom. An open kitchen and living room, hallway to bedrooms and bath.

A weekday evening. 7. JOAN and HARRY enter.

JOAN: I'm saying isn't it *reasonable* to expect that she be *competent.*

HARRY: That depends.

JOAN: No, I don't think it *does* depend. That a *minimum* level of, [you know what I'm saying,] I ask that something be Done, Can't there be one chance in *five* that it ends up being Done?

HARRY: How old is she?

JOAN: I don't know.

HARRY: Is she senile?

JOAN: is she *what?*

HARRY: Maybe she's senile, you have to adjust your expectations.

JOAN: Harry, she's Twenty.

HARRY: Woa woa woa, She's *Twenty?*

JOAN: or Thirty, somewhere in there.

HARRY: Hold on a second.

JOAN: What *difference* does it make?

HARRY: She's a *child.*

JOAN: Oh, horseshit.

HARRY: She's a *baby.*

JOAN: Please. You should see her.

HARRY: Can she vote?

JOAN: She's Twenty-*seven*, Harry, she's an Adult.

HARRY: (*Behind the kitchen counter, offering.*) [Wine or a drink drink?]

JOAN: [a drink. Bourbon.]

HARRY: [Do we *have* Bourbon?]

JOAN: [Wine, then, fine.]

HARRY: [Wine?]

JOAN: [Please.]

HARRY: She's an *intern*.

JOAN: She's an Adult Person. She's Accountable.

HARRY: She lives with her parents.

JOAN: She does not live with her parents.

HARRY: You don't know that.

JOAN: I don't *happen* to.

HARRY: Is she an intern?

JOAN: That's not relevant.

HARRY: She's an intern.

JOAN: Call it what you will.

HARRY: You fired another intern.

JOAN: If you ask a *nine* year old, would you *staple* this, I'll be back in six *hours* –

HARRY: Jo. You fired another intern.

JOAN: I was *forced* to!

HARRY: (*Handing her a glass of wine.*) People [you may not know this] an intern is a *volunteer*, practically.

JOAN: I know what one *is*.

HARRY: It's a summer *job*, Jo, she lives on pizza and *wine* coolers, she has seven roommates.

JOAN: I know what an *intern* is.

HARRY: She sleeps on a pull-out sofa.

JOAN: But when she comes to *work*, Harry, and you ask her to do something truly *menial* –

HARRY: It's *summer*.

JOAN: Is it too hot to *staple*?

HARRY: It's a summer *job*, she thinks it might be *fun*, it's work for you or does she go to *Camp*.

JOAN: She's thirty!

HARRY: You don't know how old she is.

JOAN: I don't *happen* to, –

HARRY: Is she in college?

Pause. JOAN doesn't know.

Do you know her *name*?

JOAN: Dorothy.

HARRY: Her name is *Dorothy*?

JOAN: She goes by Dot.

HARRY: *Really*?

JOAN: She's from Rochester.

HARRY: Oh Jesus Jo you fired a *Nun*, you fired a *nice* person – Was she Pregnant?

JOAN: She wasn't *competent*.

BEANE enters, quietly. He wears his overcoat. He stands just inside the door. They don't appear to notice him.

12

If. Let's say *If* [and she could be a *junkie*, by the way, you have no idea *who* she is, you defend her because *I* fired her, if I gave her a *raise*, you say she's over*paid*, you oppose me for *fun*, Harry.]

HARRY: [That's called talking.]

JOAN: [Excuse me?]

HARRY: [That's conversation, what you've just described.]

JOAN: [excuse me, *What*?]

HARRY: [If I *agreed* with you, that'd be it, you say something, I'd repeat it verbatim and then we sit in silence for the rest of our lives. That's why *Parrots* eventually drive you *insane*, the relentless Agreement.]

Pause.

JOAN: Let's say *If* [and I'm gonna ignore that last bit, to save the marriage, I'm gonna pretend you don't actually think that] Let's say a person is *asked*, I dunno five *hundred* times to do something, and say she *works* for you, you *pay* her, she *understands* that her job is to *do* things.

HARRY: Do you pay her?

JOAN: Of course.

HARRY: how much?

JOAN: Who *cares*?

HARRY: Enough to buy food? Maybe she's malnourished. People who lack protein, after a while they can't tie their shoes.

JOAN: (*To BEANE, without recognition that he has been hitherto unacknowledged.*) I'll give you fifty dollars to kill him.

HARRY: (*Also without surprise re: his presence or silence.*) Your sister fired another intern, Beane, and this one's an Innocent, from Rochester, she fired a Virgin.

BEANE crosses to a sofa. He sits.

JOAN: A Living Wage, let's say.

HARRY: What does that mean? Does she live in the street? Can she buy *clothes*?

JOAN: Which is a whole other – *Jesus, Christ, Please*: Can she keep the underwear *inside* the pants? [It's a *Style*, I understand, But are you a *Plumber*? I think it's in*appropriate*. Alright? Am I allowed to say that? Fine, I'm a *reactionary*] This is an *Office*, I have *Clients*, Am I allowed to think she shouldn't *Advertise* her Panties?

HARRY: She mooned a client?

JOAN: Practically.

HARRY: You fired her for mooning a client?

JOAN: For losing one.

HARRY: She lost a client.

JOAN: She mis*placed* it.

HARRY: a client.

JOAN: a file.

HARRY: so the underwear situation is just in addition to the losing the file situation –

JOAN: How does that HAPPEN?

HARRY: She lost a file.

JOAN: The size of a *phone*book.

HARRY: How'd she lose it.

JOAN: My first question.

HARRY: how did she.

JOAN: She *misplaced* it, apparently.

HARRY: She just lost it.

JOAN: She then *found* it.

HARRY: Where?

JOAN: In the filing thing.

HARRY: In the filing cabinet?

JOAN: Yes.

    Beat.

HARRY: So wait a second, So wait a minute: You're saying she Mis*filed* it.

JOAN: However you wanna put it.

HARRY: She misfiled it, but then she *found* it.

JOAN: I guess. (*Beat.*) what.

HARRY: You *fired* her.

JOAN: A very potentially *expensive* mistake, Harry.

HARRY: Potentially?

JOAN: I have to be able to expect a minimum level of *Competence* –

HARRY: She made a *mistake,* Jo, Jesus, you misfile something, it's the *Alphabet,* you haven't had your coffee, I can remember fucking up the alphabet –

JOAN: When you were *two.*

HARRY: She made a *mistake.*

JOAN: Which when I *corrected* her [Listen, I am *often* fair] Mistakes aren't preferable, but they *happen,* I *understand,* but when I *Correct* you, it's not *personal,* Jesus, You can't *Cry.* It's *Noon.* People are *around,* you have to have a tiny thing of *Composure.* I am *Allowed* to *speak* to you. You can't burst into *Tears.*

    Beat.

HARRY: You fired her because she cried?

Pause.

Jo.

JOAN: what.

HARRY: You fired the intern because she *cried*?

Pause.

JOAN: It was noon.

HARRY: That... Wow... – It's not what your average Mentor does in that situation.

JOAN: yeah, well.

HARRY: That's what maybe Genghis *Khan* does in that situation.

JOAN: No one does anything Harry, they read magazines and they flirt with the mail guy and then you ask them to actually file and they fuck it up and they cry, what am I supposed to do.

HARRY: How about if you stop hiring interns?

JOAN: How about if I stop hiring nincompoops.

HARRY: How about if you stop making the nincompoops cry?

JOAN: I am surrounded by incompetent cry-babies, Beane, I guess it's my cross to bear.

Beat.

BEANE: Sorry, is that a question?

HARRY: (*Leaping to his feet.*) The *thing*!

JOAN: what. Oh Jesus, the quiz thing.

HARRY: (*Crossing to the bedroom.*) It's not a *quiz.*

JOAN: The 'test' thing.

HARRY: (*From off.*) It's Diagnostic!

JOAN: (*Yelling off, to HARRY.*) It's horseshit! (*To BEANE.*) Do you even *know* about this? Did he ask you? (*Yelling off, to HARRY.*) Did you even *ask* him? (*To BEANE.*) He's got this Quiz, (*Yelling off, to HARRY.*) Did you *buy* it? (*To BEANE.*) Who has any *idea* where he *got* the thing. (*Yelling off, to HARRY.*) From a *Gumball* Machine! (*To BEANE.*) It's this totally crackpot fake-shrink – (*Yelling off, to HARRY.*) You bought it off a *Fortune* Teller! (*To BEANE.*) He's been going on about it for a *week*, how's he's going to *administer* this thing, like he's *qualified*, like he's a *clinician*, but meanwhile it's this pretend-psychology *quiz* –

HARRY: (*Returning with a stack of paper sealed in plastic wrap.*) It's guaranteed.

JOAN: By whom.

HARRY: The, I dunno, it says here: The A M D A A D A.

JOAN: What does that stand for.

HARRY: Doesn't say.

JOAN: It stands for Nothing, and you know it.

HARRY: (*To JOAN.*) How does aspirin work?

JOAN: Why?

HARRY: Do you know?

JOAN: I don't *happen* to.

HARRY: Do you take it?

JOAN: Oh please.

HARRY: See? So there you go, some things you trust.

JOAN: Not if you rip them out of *Cosmo*.

HARRY: Why are you against it?

JOAN: [Because that's what Talking is.]

HARRY: [ha.]

JOAN: [Because apparently Conversation is my opposition to your every Vowel and Consonant.]

HARRY: [not quite what I said.]

JOAN: [Because if I *agreed* with you isn't that why everyone hates Parrots.]

HARRY: [ok, funny.]

BEANE: I want to do it.

    Pause.

JOAN: (*To BEANE.*) Why?

HARRY: He wants to do it.

JOAN: Do you know what it *is*?

HARRY: It's a personality test.

JOAN: Why would he want to take a personality test?

HARRY: It could help him.

JOAN: How would it help him?

HARRY: It's Diagnostic.

JOAN: (*To BEANE.*) [Can you please make him stop saying that?]

HARRY: Why don't we get started. You ready Beane?

JOAN: (*Standing.*) I'm getting a drink. (*Muttering as she crosses to the kitchen.*) [I refuse to even, – Ripped from a *magazine*, written by an *intern*, is what it is, is some *child* had a *home*work assignment, write a *quiz*, have it in by *Tuesday* and here we are *falling* for it, not even gonna *participate*.]

HARRY: Excellent. Now. (*Unwrapping the test.*) Whattawe got. Here we are: Question One. You ready Beane?

BEANE: ok.

HARRY: Terrific. We begin. (*Reading.*) 'A scenario. It's your birthday. You are presented –'

BEANE: Happy.

Pause.

HARRY: Excuse me?

BEANE: happy.

HARRY: What's that mean?

BEANE: What does 'happy' mean?

HARRY: I haven't read the question.

JOAN: (*To BEANE.*) You have to let him read you the whole question, Beane.

HARRY: Was that your *Answer?*

BEANE: Happy.

JOAN: (*To BEANE.*) But you have to let him *finish* first.

HARRY: You have to find out what I'm actually *asking.*

JOAN: (*To HARRY.*) He understands.

HARRY: (*To BEANE.*) First I ask you the question and *then* you answer, based on what I'm actually asking you.

BEANE: That seems fair.

HARRY: Right? It's a test.

BEANE: I see.

HARRY: You do. Excellent. We proceed. Question One: 'A scenario. It's your birthday. You are presented, by your most beloved, with a gift-wrapped box. Which of the following items do you wish is inside.'

BEANE: A rainbow.

Beat.

HARRY: Jo.

JOAN: I know.

19

HARRY: (*To JOAN.*) It's multiple *choice*.

JOAN: (*To BEANE.*) It's multiple choice.

HARRY: He must have taken *tests*.

JOAN: Beane, you have to let him read the *whole* question, even if it's pointless and fraudulent.

HARRY: Thank you Jo, that's helpful.

JOAN: Sure.

HARRY: (*To BEANE.*) First you hear the *choices*, Beane, and *then*, from *those*, you choose what you want to be in the box.

BEANE: Interesting.

Beat.

HARRY: Right. Yes it is. Now here we go. You wait for the choices. Now: 'Item *One*: a puppy.'

BEANE: That seems fine.

HARRY: *Beane, Christ*, It's Multiple *Choice*. You hear *Four* Choices.

JOAN: (*Evenly.*) [Harry, if you yell at him I will come over there and I will slap you.]

HARRY: (*To JOAN.*) [He won't –]

JOAN: [If you yell at him again, if you raise your *voice*, I'm not kidding.]

Beat.

HARRY: [sorry.]

JOAN: [ok.]

HARRY: [He won't let me read all four options.]

JOAN: (*To BEANE.*) Let him finish the question please and if he yells at you I'll hit him with my fist.

BEANE: ok.

JOAN: Go ahead, Harry.

HARRY: Terrific. So Item one is a puppy, Item Two: a
Songbird. Item Three: A Bunny and item four is a baby.

Beat.

BEANE: A Human baby?

HARRY: This is the question.

BEANE: They put a baby in a wrapped box?

HARRY: apparently.

BEANE: Who would do that?

HARRY: (*Reading.*) 'Your most beloved,' it says, I guess that
would be friends and family.

BEANE: Is it alive?

Pause.

HARRY: (*To BEANE.*) What kind of question is that?

JOAN: I think we can assume it's alive, Beane.

BEANE: It can breathe?

HARRY: Yes.

BEANE: How?

HARRY: It has, I dunno, Let's just *assume*, ok? That all the gifts
are alive, just to keep this from getting *creepy*, everyone's
fine, the box has holes in the top, it's ventilated.

BEANE: How long has he been in there?

HARRY: The baby? An hour. Not even. A Minute, we just
wrapped him up just this second, I just now put the lid on.

BEANE: Is there food?

HARRY: Yes. There is food and a blanket and if it's a bunny then there's a little patch of *grass*, they *Like* it in there, Beane, they are *Comfortable*.

BEANE: They're comfortable in the box.

HARRY: Yes they are.

BEANE: Are you sure?

HARRY: Yes, because if we're ever going to get to question *two*, [out of, like, two *hundred* questions] If we're ever going to move *on*, You have to answer the *Question*, You have to *Choose*, Beane: Puppy, Bird, Bunny, Baby, Alright? Which one do you *want?*

BEANE: I'm going to say the Bird.

Beat.

HARRY: The Bird. Well there you go. That's Item Two. Excellent. See? Is that so hard? Terrific. Now: –

BEANE: That way if it's dead, at least we didn't kill the baby.

Pause.

HARRY: Beane.

BEANE: Birds die all the time.

HARRY: Beane.

BEANE: They fly into windows.

HARRY: The bird's not dead.

BEANE: It's in a wrapped box.

HARRY: There are *holes* in the top.

BEANE: The question didn't say that.

HARRY: It's *Implied.*

JOAN: How is it implied?

BEANE: I think by killing the bird, you save the life of the other three.

HARRY: No, In fact that is *not* what you do, What you *do* is you Skew the *test*, You answer the question based on a Morose Assumption, So now instead of saying what you *Like*, you have stated what you most want *Dead*, which is the *Opposite* of the *question*, so when the results are *in*, you will have the *Opposite personality* of the one you actually *Have*!

JOAN: Harry, what did I tell you.

HARRY: He's giving opposite *answers*!

JOAN: What did I say about the yelling?

HARRY: You can't choose what you want to *die*, Jo, it skews the entire *test*.

BEANE: (*Standing, crossing to the door.*) I have an appointment.

BEANE is unheard, his cross unacknowledged.

HARRY: Is it too much for him to answer the question?

JOAN: Apparently.

HARRY: Can we just *try* it where he doesn't base his answers on creepy assumptions about babies dying?

BEANE: (*At the door.*) I just remembered, I must have an appointment.

BEANE exits, closing the door behind him. Pause.

HARRY: What the hell.

Pause.

JOAN: Harry?

HARRY: He left.

JOAN: (*Holding up her empty glass, requesting.*) Harry. Bourbon.

Lights.

BEANE's apartment. Later that night.

BEANE enters. The apartment is nearly dark. Meek light from a neighboring unit allows the practiced BEANE to hang keys on a hook.

BEANE then stands unmoving, in the dark, in his coat.

Pause.

A FEMALE VOICE: You're just gonna stand there?

BEANE: (*Screams.*)

A FEMALE VOICE: It's depressing, Jesus, turn a light on.

> *The standing lamp above the tattered armchair is turned on. Brightness. The lamp sheds considerably more light than it did in Scene One. It illuminates MOLLY. She lounges, one leg thrown over the chair's arm. She wears men's clothing.*

> *BEANE puts his arms above his head, surrendering.*

MOLLY: Can I ask you something?

BEANE: (*Re: her outfit.*) Those are my pants.

MOLLY: [Put your arms down.]

BEANE: You're wearing my clothes.

MOLLY: [I said put your arms down.]

> *BEANE lowers his arms to his sides.*

And I understand the thing of Minimalism, I've seen these places, believe me, Where the entire *apartment* is *Barren* and *spotless*, you could do open-heart *surgery* on the *floor*, the place is so fucking *Sterile*, and then have this One Perfect Vase*, *Perched*, in the exact *center* of the room, some fucking *architect* with his Himalayan *Vase*, I can't tell you how many of those things I have *smashed* in my lifetime, –

---

* *Pronounced with a satiric long 'a'.*

BEANE: (*An attempt to gain her attention.*) excuse me.

MOLLY: But even *then*! Even the goddamn *Minimalists,* Give me ten *seconds* [He's got his *vase* and his skinny girlfriend and it's all so *Precise*] But gimme ten *seconds* and I will lead you to a *broom* closet *Crammed* with high school *year*books and perfumed *love* letters and stuffed *animals* from like, *infant*hood, These Fucking *People*! God *forbid* someone finds out you have a beating Heart! God *Forbid* you are seen to have *Blood,* These Goddamn ARCHITECTS! 'I have reduced my oh-so-very Busy and Complicated life to a single flawless *Vase,*' But Mark my words: Give me eight *seconds* and I will lead you *Directly* to a closet full of *sentiment*!

BEANE: excuse me.

MOLLY: But then *You.* Can I ask you a question? What kind of *life* is this?

BEANE: I think that's two questions. –

MOLLY: Look at this! (*MOLLY has a paper bag at her feet. She will pull forth BEANE's meager possessions.*) A cup. A hat. [A hideously – look at this thing, it's the hair*shirt* of hats, who would *wear* this?] Gloves. Half a tube of *tooth*paste, a toothbrush, a razor. Three pairs of identical socks. The underwear [which, ordinarily, I'm not out here liberating *briefs,* but it's slim pickings] and a Spoon. (*Beat.*) A *Single Spoon*! Can you *Explain* this to me?

BEANE: It's a spoon.

MOLLY: You Don't Have a *Fork*!

BEANE: I use the spoon.

MOLLY: You don't have a *plate*!

BEANE: I use the cup.

MOLLY: You eat out of a *Cup*?

BEANE: sometimes.

MOLLY: Who *are* you?

BEANE: I was just hoping to ask you that same –

MOLLY: Where's your *Calendar*?

BEANE: my calendar?

MOLLY: or a *Painting, Any*thing, a *Picture.*

BEANE: I guess there does seem to be a lack of –

MOLLY: Do you have any *relatives*?

BEANE: I have a sister.

MOLLY: Do you *like* her?

    Beat.

BEANE: In what way?

MOLLY: In like there might be a *picture* – [What's your name?]

    Pause.

    [What's your *name*, dammit, Do not make me ask you again.]

BEANE: [Beane.]

MOLLY: There might be a *picture*, Beane, a *Sign* that you *live* here, that you *exist* on this *planet*, you might have acquired a *Plate*.

BEANE: I have the cup.

MOLLY: Are you a monk?

BEANE: No.

MOLLY: A musician?

BEANE: I work for the city.

MOLLY: A *rich* person [This I've seen and then there's an off-shore *account* somewhere, *bulging*, but the guy lives on leftover *crumbs* and *dust*.]

BEANE: I don't have any money.

MOLLY: Who Are You?

BEANE: I'm not sure how to answer that.

MOLLY: Where's your closet full of sentimental collections?

BEANE: I don't have one.

MOLLY: Why not?

BEANE: I don't collect anything.

MOLLY: You don't not only not *Collect* anything.

BEANE: I don't have anything.

MOLLY: This is what I'm saying.

BEANE: I figure I can just as easily eat out of a cup.

MOLLY: That is not how people *are*.

BEANE: oh.

MOLLY: People go to *Europe*, they're twenty, they're in love, they steal, I dunno, an *Ashtray*, from a *café* and fifteen years later it's *ugly*, but I was in love and in Paris, you keep the Ashtray.

BEANE: I don't smoke.

MOLLY: THAT'S NOT THE POINT.

BEANE: I guess I don't collect.

MOLLY: I'm not sure you *Exist*.

BEANE: What kind of criminal did you say you were, again?

MOLLY: A *Diary*.

BEANE: I've never kept one.

MOLLY: a *pen*.

BEANE: I don't like pens.

MOLLY: EVERYONE LIKES PENS.

BEANE raises his arms once again, surrendering. A reaction to her force.

People are *Given* things [put your arms down] It's a person's Fucking *Birthday*, you give him a *gift*, someone buys you a *turtleneck.*

BEANE: I don't know a lot of people.

MOLLY: Your sister.

Pause.

She gives you sweaters, Beane, at *least* once a year, don't you lie to me.

BEANE: I throw them out.

MOLLY: why.

Pause.

You throw them out, your sister has a party, she gives you a *gift* and on the way home you throw it in the trash, it's still in the box, a perfectly decent sweater, why do you do that.

Beat.

BEANE pulls his wallet from his hip pocket, placing it carefully on the table between then.

Your wallet.

BEANE: it's got sixteen dollars.

MOLLY: Why'd you do that.

BEANE: My general rule is: whoever has you at gunpoint, give them your wallet.

MOLLY: Beane. I don't have a gun.

BEANE: I think a person can have you at gunpoint whether or not they have a gun or not.

Beat.

MOLLY: (*Pointing a finger-gun at BEANE.*) Have it your way: Where's the sappy closet?

BEANE: There is none.

MOLLY: Why.

Pause. Then MOLLY raises and cocks the finger-gun.

Tell me why.

BEANE: I think objects are deceptive.

MOLLY: In What Way.

BEANE: Sometimes a sweater tells you you're Visible, when maybe that's not the case. Glasses and candlesticks tell you to expect a party, and in my experience there's not a party. I don't want to have a fork if it's gonna lie to me.

Beat.

MOLLY: Why do you stand in the dark in your own house in your coat?

BEANE: Because the last time I turned the lights on, it made it darker.

MOLLY: It made the room darker.

BEANE: and smaller.

MOLLY: Turning the lights on did this.

BEANE: Maybe it didn't cause it, but it made it harder not to notice.

MOLLY: Have you called the super?

BEANE: I'm pretty sure it's not a super-type problem.

MOLLY: What kind of problem is it?

BEANE: Maybe it's more a problem of perspective.

Beat.

MOLLY: You're a funny one.

Pause. BEANE is encouraged by this recognition.

BEANE: Can I ask you something?

MOLLY: No.

BEANE: I see.

MOLLY: Gimme the coat.

BEANE: My coat?

MOLLY: Off with it, now, toss it over here.

BEANE removes his coat and throws it to her. BEANE is revealed to be wearing an outfit identical to MOLLY's. Same pants, same shirt.

Will you look at that. Twins. (*Donning the coat, then again with the finger-gun, pointing to the armchair.*) Come sit here. Come come, hurry up.

BEANE to the chair. MOLLY crosses to the door with the paper bag of BEANE's belongings. MOLLY stops at the door, her hand on the knob.

Pause.

Beane.

BEANE: yeah?

MOLLY: Tell me the truth, God's honest truth a second.

BEANE: ok.

MOLLY: You eat out of a *cup*?

BEANE: I do, yeah.

Beat. She is interested.

MOLLY: hunh.

MOLLY exits. Pause. BEANE sits. After a moment, the light brightens.

Lights.

SCENE FOUR

A restaurant. A couple days later.

BEANE and JOAN at lunch. In front of BEANE, a sandwich.

JOAN: I have like, what is it (*Checks her watch.*) Two O'clock,
 Jesus, How does that *happen*, I have four minutes, I'm
 sorry, the new girl is a *Dim*wit, I won't be surprised if the
 place is on *Fire* when I get back, I am a *Magnet* for *Imbeciles*,
 [Remember that dog? What was our dog's name?] *Furry*,
 Remember how Furry would come in from like fifteen
 seconds outside and we'd spend the entire *afternoon* pulling
 ticks off her? That's me with the imbeciles, I take a *walk*,
 there's a *dozen* stuck in my *hair*, My Entire *Life* I'm pulling
 them off me, I am Besieged by *Dip*shits: But anyway,
 I'll be late, so she sets fire to the city, fuck it, [what was I
 saying?] oh right, So anyway, So Harry and I were talking
 the other night, after the dead bird thing, we were thinking
 we both feel like it might be, what, Wise, if we looked into
 getting you some kind of professional, whatchamacallit,
 assistance, and listen, I understand, most of these people are
 quacks, but apparently Harry's friend knows a doctor who is
 supposed to be ok, apparently, we thought you might just
 go and talk to this guy.

Pause in which BEANE takes his first bite of the sandwich.

 It's awkward, I understand, but why don't we say it's on a
 trial basis, you talk to the guy and see how you like it.

BEANE: (*Through a mouthful.*) Jesus *Christ.*

JOAN: Beane.

BEANE: (*Re. the sandwich.*) This is *Delicious*!

JOAN: Excuse me?

BEANE: (*Offering the sandwich.*) You have to *Try* this.

 Beat.

JOAN: why.

BEANE: It's Un*believable.*

JOAN: It's a turkey sandwich.

BEANE: Is this what those *taste* like?

JOAN: Pardon me?

BEANE: What do they *put* in these things! Salad Dressing! (*Off, to a passing WAITER.*) Excuse me.

JOAN: (*To BEANE.*) What are you doing.

The WAITER approaches.

BEANE: (*To the WAITER.*) Can I have another one of these?

WAITER: Another turkey club?

BEANE: Did you make this?

WAITER: Did I personally?

JOAN: *Beane.*

BEANE: (*To JOAN.*) Do you want one? (*Then to the WAITER.*) Make it two.

JOAN: (*To the WAITER.*) Don't do that, sorry, one is fine.

BEANE: (*To the WAITER.*) Have you *tasted* this?

WAITER: The turkey club?

BEANE: (*Offering the sandwich.*) You want a bite?

WAITER: No thank you.

BEANE: Is it the *Meat?* Is that what it is? It's the *bread*, right? Flour and Yeast and fucking Fairy Dust – What's your name?

WAITER: Bill?

BEANE: Hi.

WAITER: Hi.

BEANE: Have you worked here a while?

WAITER: Three months?

BEANE: Do you like it?

WAITER: It's ok.

BEANE: You *hate* it! I knew it! You *Despise* it!

WAITER: I do sort of hate it.

BEANE: How about quitting?

WAITER: Sorry?

BEANE: Have you thought about quitting?

JOAN: *Beane.*

BEANE: (*To the WAITER.*) Walk out right now. Don't even tell anybody, Go for a swim.

WAITER: I need the money.

BEANE: Do you play an instrument?

JOAN: *Whoa,* ok. (*To the WAITER.*) Excuse me, sorry, that's fine, Can I, Can I have a second with him here please?

WAITER: Sure.

The WAITER exits. JOAN looks intently at her brother. Pause.

JOAN: Beane. [what.] First of all, lemme just –

BEANE: (*Sniffing the air.*) What *is* that?

JOAN: What is what.

BEANE: *Smell* that, what is that? (*Sniffing the air.*) Chrysanthemums!

JOAN: Are you drunk?

BEANE: There's a floating scent. Quiet. Can you *smell* that?

JOAN: No.

BEANE: (*Sniffing his own armpit.*) Is that *me*? I haven't had a chance to shower in a couple of days.

JOAN: Why.

BEANE: Plus I lost my other clothes.

JOAN: What do you mean, you Lost them.

BEANE: In an incident.

JOAN: What kind of Incident?

BEANE: Shh, Jo, *Smell* that. Where is that *coming* from? (*Rising, crossing to JOAN.*) It's *you*, you fragrant sister!

JOAN: What are you doing, Get away from me.

BEANE sniffs JOAN's neck.

BEANE: Chrysanthemums! Au Natur*el*!*

JOAN: Will you sit down?

BEANE: (*Leaning in.*) Lemme get another sniff.

JOAN: (*Standing suddenly.*) *Sit Down.* (*Beat.*) *Sit*, I'm not kidding. You smell me again I'm gonna do something.

BEANE returns to his chair, unchastened.

Now:

BEANE: (*Blithely.*) So tell me. How are you, How's Harry, How's work.

Pause.

JOAN: Lemme smell your breath.

BEANE: ok.

JOAN leans toward him, he exhales.

What's it smell like?

JOAN: Turkey.

BEANE: Lemme smell yours.

* *French*

JOAN: No.

BEANE: Come on, fair's fair.

JOAN: If you're a drug addict, if you're on Narcotics, I am not joking, I'm gonna strangle you.

BEANE: Can I ask you a question?

JOAN: No.

BEANE: Do you know any songs by heart?

Beat.

JOAN: You know what I should do? I should make you pee in this glass.

BEANE: (*Standing.*) Ok.

JOAN: SIT DOWN.

BEANE sits. Pause.

BEANE: Try a bite of this sucker, you can't believe how delicious.

JOAN: I Don't Want a Bite of your Fucking *Sandwich.*

BEANE: okidoke.

JOAN: If you *sniff* me again, if you offer me another *Bite* of that thing, if you *engage* that *waiter* again, I am going to *Leap* over this table.

BEANE: He seemed like a nice guy I thought.

JOAN: Do *not* say that, do *not* say someone seems like a nice guy because this is what I'm *talking* about, that is *not* a *thought* that you would *have*, Beane, I will drag you kicking and *screaming* to a pharmacy, and I will *personally watch* you pee and I will have it Analyzed, I am *not* kidding.

WAITER: (*Having returned.*) Excuse me.

JOAN: What do *You* want?

WAITER: The second sandwich, is that to go?

BEANE: I'd like to have it here.

WAITER: ok.

BEANE: I'm starving.

WAITER: sure.

BEANE: And a beer.

WAITER: You'd like a beer?

BEANE: and a glass of tequila.

WAITER: and a beer?

BEANE: please, Bill.

WAITER: What kind of beer would you like?

BEANE: Bring me the biggest kind.

WAITER: I'll see what I can do.

BEANE: and Bill?

WAITER: Yes?

BEANE: I'd like a cupcake.

JOAN: (*To the WAITER.*) That's *enough*. Excuse me, Go away. [It's your job, I understand, I apologize] We have something of a *situation*, do me a favor, I'll over-tip, go away and don't come back.

Beat.

WAITER: Fine.

WAITER exits. Pause.

JOAN: Now.

BEANE: Yes.

JOAN: Beane.

BEANE: Joan.

JOAN: What am I going to say to you.

BEANE: I'm not sure.

JOAN: I am going to say that if I had a *Straight*jacket in my *purse*, I'd be wrestling you to the *ground*. If I carried Mace, right *now* would be the time.

BEANE: I quit my job.

JOAN: (*Reaching into her purse for her cell phone.*) Fine, that's plenty. I'm calling Harry.

BEANE: I didn't like it.

JOAN: So *What.*

BEANE: I all of sudden realized I didn't like doing it.

JOAN: Listen.

BEANE: It was really boring.

JOAN: You were *employed.*

BEANE: in a token booth.

JOAN: Do you realize how Late I am by the way?

BEANE: I met someone.

> *Pause.*

> Jo.

JOAN: Not *God*, I'm hoping, this isn't some *conversion* thing, I swear, I'll tell Mom.

BEANE: Jo.

JOAN: what.

BEANE: I think I met someone.

> *Lights.*

SCENE FIVE

BEANE's apartment.

BEANE enters. The apartment is dark. The meek light from the neighboring unit is out.

BEANE stands unmoving, in the dark. He listens intensely for any sound, hoping.

BEANE: I hold my breath to try and hear you. I get dizzy, trying to hear if you're here.

Beat.

'So turn on the light,' I realize, is the obvious thing.

Beat.

But what if I'm alone?

Beat.

you're easier to believe in with the lights off.

Beat.

We used to leave out cookies for Santa. and a carrot. It seemed to work, He always came. If I left you an offering by the fireplace, Would you come back?

Beat.

I don't have a cookie. I don't have anything. What if I left you my Hand?

Beat.

If I chewed off my hand, put it out overnight, on a plate by the mantle, Would that bring you back to me?

MOLLY: (*In darkness, from the armchair.*) Do you know who I am?

BEANE: holy shit.

*MOLLY switches on the standing lamp. It's bright. MOLLY wears
BEANE's shirt, pants and overcoat.*

hi.

Pause.

Can I get you a drink?

MOLLY: No.

BEANE: ok.

MOLLY: I will *take* one if I want one, I will Help Myself.

BEANE: There's, – I guess technically nothing, there's water
but there's no glasses.

MOLLY: What's Wrong with you?

BEANE: How do you mean?

MOLLY: No one *prays* for my return, Beane, I am not *Wished*
for. People buy *guard* Dogs and move to the *Suburbs*, people
are *Scared* of me.

BEANE: Why?

MOLLY: Because I tie them up with *phone* cord and tape their
fucking *mouths* shut, because I steal their televisions and
terrify their *children.*

BEANE: I'm glad you came back.

MOLLY: HOW IS THAT POSSIBLE?

BEANE: I like you.

MOLLY: I *Robbed* you. I took everything you had and I *sold* it,
for six *dollars.* I bought a *cheeseburger.* I ate it standing *up.*

BEANE: I don't care.

MOLLY: You should.

BEANE: I never liked any of that stuff.

39

MOLLY: Do you understand who I *am*? The last one? The architect? I took his stereo, I Ripped it out of his bookcase, It has no *buttons* and it's also a *satellite* and a particle *accelerator* and no decent person could possibly afford this *Object* and I am *Ripping* it out of his bookcase, I've got my *boot* on a *shelf* for *leverage*: but then I notice something: hold on a minute. None of the books have been read. No cracked bindings, Beane. Not a wrinkle. I burned his house down. I got some gasoline and a blowtorch and my vengeance and I burned it to the ground. I waited for him to come home and I watched the architect cry and I felt happy for the only time this year. is who I *am*.

BEANE: I think that's reasonable.

MOLLY: IT IS NOT REASONABLE.

BEANE: I would've done the same thing.

MOLLY: I BURNED HIS *HOUSE* DOWN, I COULD HAVE *KILLED* SOMEBODY.

BEANE: I hate architects.

MOLLY: (*Rising.*) Alright, Put your hands up.

BEANE: No.

MOLLY: Excuse me?

BEANE: I'd prefer not to.

MOLLY: Listen. HEY. [Are you *Suicidal*?] Put. Your Hands in the AIR.

BEANE: make me.

Pause.

MOLLY: You seem to lack a basic understanding of the situation.

BEANE: You're frightening?

MOLLY: I am capable of torrential violence.

BEANE: No, I understand.

MOLLY: My picture – excuse me, My *Visage* inspires Grown Men to Crap their *Pants*.

BEANE: impressive.

MOLLY: On *More* than one occasion.

BEANE: You're Terrifying.

MOLLY: I have broken *bones* with a *Glance*, Made Men *Bleed* with a *Word*.

BEANE: You're fearsome.

MOLLY: I have caused Hemorrhages and Hematoma.

BEANE: You're pitiless.

MOLLY: I am the stuff of *Fiction*! of *Nightmares*, I am Force without Conscience, and Given This, *What, CONCEIVABLY, WHAT* am I doing with this Cup?

MOLLY removes BEANE's cup from her coat pocket, she holds it out. Pause.

BEANE: my cup.

Pause.

MOLLY: Can I ask you a personal question?

BEANE: sure.

Pause.

MOLLY: Why do I have this in my pocket?

BEANE: Did you put it there?

MOLLY: Why do I sit on the bus with a cup in my pocket and touch it in secret?

Beat.

BEANE: You do that?

41

MOLLY: What's wrong with me?

BEANE: I think Nothing.

MOLLY: I am woeful.

BEANE: Why do you say that?

MOLLY: (*Holding up the cup.*) Look. I rubbed the enamel off
the side here. That's not how a grown person acts Beane,
Especially one as reviled as I am. I sit in the dark and I *sing*
to the thing, I'm telling you, it's a sickness.

Pause.

BEANE: You sing to my cup?

MOLLY: I don't know who I am.

Pause.

Beane?

BEANE: yeah?

MOLLY: I feel a riotous urge.

BEANE: What kind?

MOLLY: Will you do me a favor?

BEANE: ok.

MOLLY: Will you put your hands in the air?

*BEANE slowly raises his hands, surrendering. MOLLY crosses to
him. MOLLY kisses him.*

Lights.

SCENE SIX

JOAN and HARRY's apartment.

The next evening.

JOAN: You do realize that most kidnappings, it always turns out to be the person them*selves,* half the time, who kidnapped themselves.

HARRY: Can I figure out what that means. (*Beat.*) Nope.

JOAN: (*For the millionth time.*) What time is it?

HARRY: (*Approximating.*) Nine.

JOAN: What time *exactly,* Harry, please don't torture me.

HARRY: (*Looking at his watch.*) It's Nine-oh-six and what, forty seconds.

JOAN: He's *late.*

HARRY: What time was he supposed to be here?

JOAN: Before this.

HARRY: ah.

JOAN: Half the *planet* is Rabid, you act like this isn't true, Your average person sees weakness in somebody? they begin to *salivate.*

HARRY: What's your concern, exactly.

JOAN: (*Re: her wine glass.*) [How did this get empty?]

Pause.

[Harry. How did this get empty?]

HARRY: [Evaporation?]

JOAN: [Or maybe you *teased* me with a Smidgeonly Pour. Maybe you skimped.]

HARRY: [I'm exercising quality control.]

JOAN: (*Extending her glass to HARRY, who takes it.*) [Well don't. To the brim this time, seriously.]

HARRY: You think she *kidnapped* him?

JOAN: I think people are evil.

HARRY: you do not.

JOAN: I think *some* people are *very* evil, so on average, I think everyone is partly evil.

HARRY: (*Pouring.*) [You really want this *full*?]

JOAN: [Yes.] For every four brownie-baking nice people, there's one Brutal Savage, so if you use Math, everyone ends up capable of kidnapping.

HARRY: (*Carrying a very full glass to JOAN.*) [Look at that sucker, there must be a quart of wine in there.]

JOAN: [Thank you.] and plus, you might as well paint a target on the guy's forehead, if I was a psychopath, the first person I'm calling to like, *practice* on is my brother.

HARRY: You think she's torturing him?

JOAN: What time is it?

HARRY: (*Approximating.*) Ten after.

JOAN: Harry, *please*, what time is it *really*.

HARRY: (*Looking at his watch.*) Eight after and twenty-three seconds.

JOAN: thank you.

HARRY: [*Jesus.*]

JOAN: Because Who *Is* She, for *One* thing.

HARRY: Who *is* she, actually?

JOAN: Who *Knows*.

HARRY: He wouldn't tell you.

JOAN: He's gone *Loony*, try getting a *Fact* out of him, I *dare* you, if he ever *gets* here, What time is it?

HARRY: [Jo.]

JOAN: What time is it, Harry, come on, Tell me what time it is.

HARRY: [I just can't do it, Jo, honestly, I can't look at the watch again.]

Beat.

JOAN: [That's fair.]

HARRY: [I think there has to be a limit.]

JOAN: [I understand.]

HARRY: [Thank you.]

JOAN: (*Standing.*) [I'll check the stove.]

HARRY: What's her name?

JOAN: Molly.

HARRY: Molly what.

JOAN: A Reasonable Question, right? Not a *Prying* question, not a *Snooping* question, a Reasonable Fucking Everyday Fucking Question.

HARRY: He wouldn't tell you.

JOAN: Who knows if he even *knows.*

HARRY: What does she do?

JOAN: Ah. She's a 'liberator.'

HARRY: He said that?

JOAN: What could that *mean*?

HARRY: He said that?

JOAN: He *screamed* it.

HARRY: Is this before or after you fainted?

JOAN: I did not Faint.

HARRY: Before or after you suddenly lost consciousness?

JOAN: I'm calling the police.

HARRY: Good idea.

JOAN: (*Crossing to phone.*) I am, I'm not kidding.

HARRY: Really?

JOAN: He's *hours* late, Harry, he could be chained to a *radiator*.

HARRY: Except that he's not.

JOAN: You don't know that.

HARRY: You're actually calling the *police*?

JOAN: (*Picking up the phone, dialing.*) She's pulling out his *teeth* with a pair of *pliers*, for all we know. (*Into the phone.*) Hi, yeah, I need to report a what's-his-face. (*Beat.*) What's that thing called, *Ascension*. (*Beat.*) You know what? I just realized, I meant to dial a whole different, – I meant to call a friend of mine, actually, who happens to be a cop, a police-friend, so I guess I got mixed up, sorry, wrong number.

JOAN hangs up. Beat.

HARRY: Did you eat today?

JOAN: Harry, he's out of his *Mind*.

HARRY: I'm thinking it runs in the family.

JOAN: [You know what? You're an Underminer in times of serious instability, is what you are, OK?]

HARRY: Maybe he's *happy*.

JOAN: Wait 'til you see him.

HARRY: What. He's perky.

JOAN: [Perky.] Harry. Listen Closely. He was *Verbose.*

Beat.

HARRY: ...and?

JOAN: Harry!

HARRY: you're saying you've never seen that.

JOAN: Never *Seen* it! When he was twelve? [Have I told you this?] This kid Larry Somebody? On the bus, apparently, for an entire *Year*, this kid was poking Beane with a *pencil.*

HARRY: He what?

JOAN: In the *neck.*

HARRY: Come on.

JOAN: Peck peck peck, apparently, Larry Somebody, for a *year.*

HARRY: In the neck?

JOAN: Never drawing blood, just sitting behind him, *pecking* him in the neck on the bus.

HARRY: *Who* did this?

JOAN: Larry Michaelson.

HARRY: What kind of fucking *sadist.*

JOAN: and Beane never *said* anything.

HARRY: He never said anything?

JOAN: Not a *word.*

HARRY: He didn't confront the kid.

JOAN: He Never *Acknowledged* it.

HARRY: You're kidding.

JOAN: He never turned *around*!

HARRY: That, – He never *acknowledged* this kid poking him with a *pencil*?

JOAN: The truth.

HARRY: That is just *awful*.

JOAN: For a *year*.

HARRY: with the kid poking him in the *neck*?

JOAN: Like it's not *Happening*! For a fucking *school*year!

HARRY: What did your mother say?

JOAN: He never *told* her.

HARRY: Oh, that is just dis*turbing*.

JOAN: I'm *telling* you, I finally find out from this little *girl*, but it's like, *April*, and by that point, I don't even wanna calculate how much *poking* that is.

HARRY: [That whole time, he's just weathering the poking, that is just stomach-turning.]

JOAN: He never *says* anything.

HARRY: [Just makes you feel *ill*.]

JOAN: Harry, He Never *Says Anything*.

HARRY: Ah, but now he *is*, you're saying.

JOAN: He's Verbose!

HARRY: right.

JOAN: What must she be *doing* to him?

    Beat.

HARRY: [Are you *sure* there's a link between the pencil thing and this thing?]

JOAN: [Don't you undermine, Harry.]

HARRY: [Yeah but are you sure she's *torturing* him?]

JOAN: *Yes.*

> *BEANE enters. He is somewhat disheveled. Coatless and tousled.*
> *There is, perhaps, a button missing from his shirt, something*
> *askew hair-wise. BEANE crosses to the refrigerator and begins*
> *to rummage as he speaks.*

BEANE: Have I Eaten in this *Life*time? Is there *proof* that I
have *Ever* Eaten *Anything*? I am RAVISHING. I could eat a
fucking *horse* – fucking eat a *horse* – eat fucking a *horse* – *any*
of those, I was thinking on the way over, I'm lucky I didn't
walk by any *meat*, I'm likely to drop down and eat a live
dog, I'm half-ready to grab a pigeon out of the *air* and eat
its Breast.

> *Beat.*

JOAN: (*To HARRY.*) [This is what I'm talking about.]

HARRY: You hungry Beane?

BEANE: *Emancipated.*

HARRY: How's that?*

BEANE: (*Holding a carton of Chinese noodles.*) Can I eat this? Is
there a fork? (*Then spying the bottle on the counter.*) Wine!
'I am a Fool for wine, my friends, a Foolish Nit!'† Can I
drink this? I was talking to somebody the other day about
the Redundancy of Glassware, (*Offering the bottle.*) [sorry,
Does anybody want any? No?] About the *Conspiracy*, really,
of the redundancy of just about *everything*, you know, You
buy a glass thing to pour something *from* a glass thing *into*,
when, there you are *with* a glass thing, cheers. (*BEANE*
drinks from the wine bottle.) Raincoats, You *buy* a water
resistant thing when you are in fact *already* a water resistant
thing, like we're gonna make a *purchase* that's gonna
improve on *skin*, my *Ass*, I will walk naked down the street
and I will show you something about Water Repellence!

---

* *As in, 'What did you say?'*

† *Done as a quote, but it's not a quote.*

(*He then eats noodles from the carton with his hands.*) It's a Conspiracy, The Goddamn Oligarchy that *insists* we *Buy* things, Look at this: Eat a noodle *from* a carton, when you already *are* a noodle eating a noodle from a carton! 'It is foolish food, my friends, when a noodle eats a noodle!'

Beat.

JOAN: (*To HARRY.*) *You* talk to him.

HARRY: How're you doing, Beane.

BEANE: (*Blithely.*) Fine. Hungry. (*Offering the food.*) You sure you don't want any of this?

JOAN: [I'm getting a drink.]

BEANE: (*To HARRY.*) Can I borrow some money?

JOAN: (*To HARRY.*) No.

HARRY: You want to borrow money?

BEANE: please.

HARRY: How much do you need?

BEANE: How much do you have?

JOAN: Do *not* give him money.

HARRY: Why not?

JOAN: Because there are certain charities which are *worthy* and certain charities that are run by the in*sane* and you may think you're supporting the *symphony* but in fact someone's buying *amphetamines* and *rifles*.

Beat.

BEANE: (*To JOAN.*) Are you ok?

HARRY: She's concerned, Beane.

BEANE: I was gonna buy a shirt.

JOAN: Why.

BEANE: This one smells.

JOAN: *Why.*

BEANE: I've had it on for a while.

JOAN: *Why.*

BEANE: (*A thought occurs. BEANE begins to strip.*) Hey, you have a washer, plus these pants could probably use a soak. –

JOAN: BEANE. (*Beat.*) If you take your clothes off in my house if I *glimpse* your naked penis I am going to *converge* on you with this corkscrew there will be *blood,* I'm not kidding.

BEANE: (*Continuing the strip.*) We're related.

JOAN: STOP. [Give him the money Harry, now.]

HARRY: (*Pulling out his wallet, asking BEANE.*) Is fifty okay?

BEANE: How much is in there?

HARRY: One, lemme see, one-twenty?

BEANE: Can I have all of it?

HARRY: Really?

JOAN: Give it to him, Harry.

HARRY: (*To JOAN.*) Really?

JOAN: Now.

HARRY: (*To himself while handing over the money.*) [Jesus. seems like a lot.]

BEANE: (*Accepting the money.*) Thanks.

HARRY: (*To BEANE, confidentially.*) [Doesn't it seem like a lot?]

BEANE: (*To HARRY, confidentially.*) [It *is* a lot.]

HARRY: [Right?]

BEANE: [I was surprised you gave it to me.]

HARRY: [I thought she was going to kill you.]

BEANE: [You think she really would've attacked me?]

HARRY: [I think she might have actually tried to *kill* you.]

BEANE: [She does seem a little hot under the collar.]

HARRY: [You're telling *me*.]

BEANE: [Has she *been* like this?]

HARRY: [She thinks you're in a cult.]

JOAN: Excuse me.

BEANE: [a cult?]

JOAN: I can *hear* you.

HARRY: [She says you've been verbose.]

BEANE: [Did she tell you about the fainting?]

JOAN: I did not *faint.*

HARRY: [You do seem a touch talkative, I have to concur.]

JOAN: a Touch *Talkative*?

BEANE: (*Beginning a kind of confession.*) Hey Harry?

HARRY: Yes?

BEANE: Can I tell you something?

HARRY: Alright.

BEANE: Do you have a second?

HARRY: Sure.

BEANE: Do you know that thing about the better mousetrap?

HARRY: What. The saying?

BEANE: The *saying*, Exactly.

HARRY: Sure, what is it, you build a better mousetrap, something something path to your door.

BEANE: I think I understand that now.

HARRY: How do you mean.

BEANE: I've been thinking about it.

HARRY: You didn't understand the phrase.

BEANE: I always thought, Why Bother?

HARRY: I see.

JOAN: (*Scoffing.*) [you see, please.]

BEANE: They work *fine,* I thought, The mice are *dead,* What's the point?

HARRY: Now you think you know the point.

BEANE: I realized what the point is.

HARRY: What's that.

BEANE: It's sexual intercourse.

JOAN: [oh for the love of God.]

BEANE: I realized that building mousetraps has nothing to do with catching mice.

HARRY: You think that phrase is about the what, the notion of...... I guess, what:

BEANE: I think it's about fucking.

HARRY: I see.

BEANE: Can I tell you something?

HARRY: I hesitate here, Beane.

BEANE: Skyscrapers?

HARRY: Skyscrapers.

BEANE: I thought: *Jesus,* Leave the sky *alone.*

HARRY: I see.

JOAN: [You do not *see,* Harry, stop saying you see.]

BEANE: That we should *scrape* the Heavens, who thinks like that? Could he be eating what I'm eating? I was sure there was a Secret. These people must get more oxygen, they were fortified from birth, they somehow weren't *embarrassed* by themselves.

HARRY: Builders, you're talking about.

BEANE: All of them, Coopers, the whole group of them.

JOAN: (*To HARRY.*) [Coopers. Say you see now, smart guy.]

BEANE: I saw all this *Living,* People going to work and recreating and Why are all they all so willing? I watched them from my apartment, through my peephole, I watched them skipping down the hall and I wondered what kind of *shoes* they wore, to make them *want* things so much. and when I went outside, I took the peephole with me. I stood behind my door and I watched them in the park. I didn't understand them, playing hopscotch and writing formulas, building ships from kits and taking walks and I wonder if I can whip up the desire to *eat.* They scared me, Harry, I hid behind my door and I looked at them through a tiny hole. I couldn't imagine what made people so *shameless.* What secret ingredient makes you think things are Possible?

HARRY: I don't know.

BEANE: It's sexual intercourse, Harry. The secret is Fucking.

JOAN: (*Rejecting her wine.*) [Alright. You know what? Bourbon.]

BEANE: Hey Harry?

HARRY: That's a helluva theory there, Beane.

BEANE: (*To HARRY.*) Can I ask you something personal?

JOAN: No.

BEANE: When you first met my sister?

JOAN: Woa woa woa *Woa.*

BEANE: Do you remember what she smelled like?

JOAN: Excuse me, No, Do not answer that Harry, that is not appropriate.

HARRY: (*To BEANE.*) What she *smelled* like?

BEANE: When you first met.

JOAN: Harry, don't encourage him, That is not a question, It's an exercise in Shenanigans.

HARRY: Melon.

Beat.

JOAN: What?

HARRY: (*To BEANE.*) She smelled like melon.

JOAN: (*To BEANE.*) He's kidding.

HARRY: (*To JOAN.*) I'm not, actually.

JOAN: I smelled like a *melon?*

HARRY: Like a really ripe cantaloupe.

JOAN: Are you serious?

HARRY: You did, yeah.

JOAN: And you *remember* that?

HARRY: Vividly. Jesus, I still, in the Summer sometimes, on a really hot day when I pass a fruit stand...

Pause.

JOAN: excuse me?

Pause.

Harry? What happens when you pass a fruit stand?

HARRY: I dunno, I end up, you know, with a little a bit of a situation in my pants.

Beat.

BEANE: THAT IS WHAT I AM *TALKING* ABOUT!

JOAN: *Harry!*

HARRY: [I can't believe I just admitted that.]

JOAN: From a *fruit* stand?

HARRY: [I can't believe I just *said* that.]

JOAN: You get a…a *situation* from smelling a *melon*?

HARRY: Yeah. or I guess from a certain, I dunno, *episode* which the melon smell reminds me of.

JOAN: Harry, you *Rascal.*

HARRY: [Can we talk about this later?]

JOAN: From an Episode? You *Scala*wag! Which episode?

BEANE: BUILD A BETTER MOUSETRAP!

JOAN: I am *wow*, how long ago *was* that, you remember one specific time? Which time?

HARRY: [I'll tell you later.]

BEANE: (*Standing, presenting himself.*) Look.

JOAN: Which episode?

BEANE: I've been wiped clean.

JOAN: (*To HARRY.*) That time at my mother's house?

HARRY: Jo, He's been wiped clean.

JOAN: What does that mean?

BEANE: The smudge on my sight is gone.

JOAN: (*To BEANE.*) Does this have to do with the fruit stand thing?

BEANE: Where I once walked under a low looming sky, now those same clouds hold Water for the frogs and the flowers. Where once I whiffed shit and smelled the decay and death in it, now it's Fertilizer: Grow tomatoes, eat them, feed your friends. Once I heard a wall of sound, an oppressive wave of sirens and screaming, indistinguishable, Now across a crowded street I hear the crisp 'snick' of a kid opening a soda, I hear his gulp-gulp and his satisfied 'aah.' Once the water in my glass tasted like rotted pipes and base metals. Now, it's see-through Joy. Hydrogen and oxygen. It's two 'h's and an 'o', a molecular *menage à trois,* I taste love and sex in every sip. (*Beat.*) I met my Molly and I can taste the sweet salt of her sweat and I can see her clearly in the dark. I can hear her every whispered vowel and I can feel her hands on my ass. (*Beat.*) Harry, Jo, Look. I'm brand new.

Lights.

SCENE SEVEN

JOAN and HARRY's apartment.

The next morning. A weekday. JOAN and HARRY in bathrobes.

JOAN regards the phone.

JOAN: I can't do it.

HARRY: You can absolutely do it.

JOAN: I'm a terrible liar.

HARRY: You are a magnificent liar.

JOAN: am I?

HARRY: Of course you are.

JOAN: What do I *say*?

HARRY: You're sick and you can't come in.

JOAN: Is that all it is?

HARRY: (*Handing JOAN the phone.*) It's a cinch. Here.

   Pause. JOAN regards the phone.

JOAN: You know how many times I've cursed the people who
   do this?

HARRY: a million?

JOAN: Now here I am doing it, I can't believe it.

HARRY: You're a convert to the world of lying and sloth,
   – [Jesus *Christ*, Jo.]

   Beat.

JOAN: [what.]

HARRY: [*Wow.*]

JOAN: [what.]

HARRY: [Have you *always* had that?]

JOAN: [The robe?]

HARRY: [Where'd you get that?]

JOAN: [I dunno, I stole it from some hotel, why.]

HARRY: [Jesus *Christ.*]

JOAN: [You like it?]

HARRY: [It's not a thing of liking it, it's a thing of The Fucking Robe Makes My Insides Hurt.]

JOAN: (*Flattered.*) [Get outta town.]

HARRY: [I am not kidding.]

JOAN: [Don't I always wear this?]

HARRY: [It's a thing of the Robe is *Tantalizing.*]

JOAN: [Really?]

HARRY: [It's a thing of what is it *made* of, it's like someone harvested, harvested my *soul* and then took a *loom* and with the fabric, I guess with the fabric of my soul they made a robe, and then there you are wearing my soul except of course technically it's actually still a *robe.*]

Beat.

JOAN: [Honey, I'm sorry, I'm not sure what that means.]

HARRY: [I got lost halfway through there.]

JOAN: [It got away from you a little bit.]

HARRY: [I'm not used to talking like that, it just sort of ran away from me.]

JOAN: [You like the robe.]

HARRY: [That was my point.]

JOAN: [I got that part.]

HARRY: [that seeing it on you makes me want to take it off you.]

Beat.

JOAN: [see now that I understand.]

HARRY: [Right?]

JOAN: Gimme that phone, hand that fucking thing over here.

HARRY: (*Handing her the phone.*) You're gonna do it?

JOAN: Yes I am. (*Beat. Handing it back.*) Right after you.

HARRY: You want me to go?

JOAN: It makes me *nervous*, I don't *know* why, It's like I'm cutting *class* and smoking pot and tricking my mother, it is very *Exciting*.

HARRY: (*Dialing.*) [I love this, once a week we should do this, the rest of the world calls in sick every other *day*, we should –] (*Into the phone.*) Kate. (*Then, holding his nose to sound congested.*) Kate, hi it's Harry, listen, I've got this, I don't know what it is, something bronchial, it's really terrible. (*Beat.*) Oh you're sweet, could you? That would be great. (*Beat.*) I know, plenty of fluids. (*A fake sneeze.*) (*Beat.*) Thanks, God bless you too. (*HARRY hangs up.*)

Beat.

JOAN: *Harry.*

HARRY: Right?

JOAN: God bless you too?

HARRY: Was that too much?

JOAN: You blessed her right back.

HARRY: Did that work?

JOAN: and the *sneeze.*

HARRY: Was the sneeze good?

JOAN: Who knew the husband was so talented?

HARRY: (*Handing JOAN the phone.*) Throw one into *your* thing.

JOAN: Should I?

HARRY: *Hell* yes, give it a little panache.

JOAN: [Doesn't this feel like high school?]

HARRY: [I love it.]

JOAN: [We should be smoking cigarettes and making out on the sofa.]

HARRY: [Let's get some cigarettes.]

JOAN: [Who was the first girl you ever kissed?]

HARRY: [You.]

JOAN: [Shut up.]

HARRY: [I saved myself.]

JOAN: (*Dialing.*) [You are so full of malarkey. Me.]

HARRY: Throw the sneeze in there!

JOAN: (*Dialing.*) I'm gonna toss in a whopper, watch this, I am gonna sneeze her into *oblivion* – (*Into the phone, holding her nose to sound congested.*) Louise? (*Fake sneeze.*) It's me. (*Fake sneeze.*)

HARRY: [Very nice.]

JOAN: (*Into the phone.*) I'm sick.

HARRY: [Sure, great, get right to the point.]

JOAN: (*Into the phone.*) I've got something bad.

HARRY: [Perfect.]

JOAN: (*Into the phone.*) I'm not sure. Something very bad.

HARRY: [Maybe try and get a little more *specific*.]

JOAN: (*Into the phone.*) I think it might be tubuncular.*

HARRY: [Excellent, there you go, sounds serious.]

JOAN: (*Fake sneeze.*)

HARRY: [Could lead to tubunculosis.]

JOAN: (*Into the phone.*) No, I already called, they said it's a twenty-four hour thing.

HARRY: [Short term tubunculosis.]

JOAN: (*Into the phone.*) From food, apparently.

HARRY: [Careful Jo, you don't wanna get too medical.]

JOAN: (*Into the phone.*) I'm not sure, I did have a tuna sandwich.

HARRY: [See now you're gonna get yourself in trouble.]

JOAN: (*Into the phone.*) Oh no, that's okay, don't come by.

HARRY: [Oh shit, time to hang up.]

JOAN: (*Into the phone.*) They said it's contagious.

HARRY: [Maybe just do the sneeze again.]

JOAN: (*Into the phone.*) It's a plague.

HARRY: [A *plague*? Jo hang up, seriously.]

JOAN: (*Into the phone.*) I doubt it'd be in the paper, they're trying to keep it from spreading.

HARRY: [Oh Jesus.]

JOAN: (*Into the phone.*) Louise? I feel a surge coming on, I better go take a shot. a thing. a Shot, a Pill, a Thing. (*Fake sneeze.*)

JOAN hangs up the phone. Pause.

* *Too-BUNK-yoo-ler.*

HARRY: wow.

JOAN: I told you.

HARRY: That is some *terrible* lying.

JOAN: I told you.

HARRY: But that is some *dreadful* lying.

JOAN: The tuna sandwich part?

HARRY: You got, [what was it?] Tubunculosis from a tuna *sandwich*?

JOAN: I know.

HARRY: That is some *Hellacious* lying.

JOAN: I think she believed me.

HARRY: Is that *possible*?

JOAN: You know what? I don't *care. (Into the phone. She does not dial, there's no one there, it's a gesture.)* I don't even *like* tuna, you moron, I'm staying home to smoke cigarettes and make out with my husband.

She hangs up the phone. Beat.

HARRY: Congratulations.

JOAN: Thank you.

HARRY: How do you feel.

JOAN: *(Positively.)* I feel......Slack.

HARRY: Welcome to the human race.

Pause.

JOAN: So now what.

HARRY: Now we play hooky.

JOAN: Right. *(Beat.)* So what does that involve.

HARRY: I have no idea.

Pause.

JOAN: Isn't there a lot of Lounging?

HARRY: I've heard that.

JOAN: You slump.

HARRY: That sounds right.

JOAN: You wear sweatpants.

HARRY: How's this?

HARRY lounges deeply.

JOAN: Harry, you are multi-faceted.

HARRY: Do I seem idle?

JOAN: Very.

HARRY: How's my posture?

JOAN: Dreadful.

HARRY: Thank you. (*Sitting up.*) You try.

JOAN: Watch this.

JOAN lounges, stiffly, determinedly. Beat.

How'm I doing.

HARRY: Not well.

JOAN: (*An attempt at Method Hooky.*) 'I am Irresponsible.' How's that?

HARRY: It's a little Energetic.

JOAN: 'Who gives a shit? Not me. I am whistling Dixie, Flunk me out of gradeschool.'

Beat.

HARRY: It could be a little more lackluster.

JOAN: (*Standing.*) *Fuck.* This is not *easy*, Harry, you'd think it'd be Easy.

HARRY: Who knew?

JOAN: There must be a *trick.*

HARRY: Booze.

JOAN: *Yes.*

HARRY: I'll get you a drink.

JOAN: An actual drink?

HARRY: Don't you want one?

JOAN: Isn't it eight-thirty in the morning?

HARRY: Technically.

JOAN: I haven't had coffee, I think I might puke. Those Fuckers with their precious hooky Secrets!

   Beat.

HARRY: (*Handing her an imaginary glassful.*) Here.

JOAN: what is it?

HARRY: Liquor.

JOAN: Do you think I should?

HARRY: Bottoms up.

JOAN: (*She drinks.*) *Jesus* that is strong.

HARRY: It's double proof.

   Beat.

JOAN: I'm still feeling a little *punctual.*

HARRY: Try this.

HARRY removes the belt from JOAN's robe. He ties her off. He rolls up her sleeve and mimes a needle into her arm.

I think you need the full wallop.

Beat.

Anything?

JOAN: *woa.*

HARRY: Is it working?

JOAN: I feel a little good-for-nothing.

HARRY: That's encouraging.

JOAN: Burn My Calendar. I am Unavailable!

HARRY: Try some lounging.

JOAN: (*She sits, loosey-goosey.*) woo! sofa cushions.

HARRY: I think it's kicking in.

JOAN: I am fucked the fuck up.

HARRY: There's some hooky dialect if I ever heard any.

JOAN: Can I have a cigarette?

HARRY: (*Handing her an imaginary.*) Sure.

JOAN: Thank you.

HARRY: might have one myself.

JOAN: Can you blow a smoke ring?

HARRY: Watch this: I'll write your name. (*He does, in one exhalation.*)

JOAN: That's a duck.

HARRY: That's what I meant.

JOAN: *Harry.*

HARRY: what.

JOAN: Look at your *hair*line.

HARRY: Pardon?

JOAN: It's Magnificent!

HARRY: That has gotta be the junk talking.

JOAN: I have a confession.

HARRY: Stoned confessions are a hooky staple.

JOAN: You know what I wish?

HARRY: I could not guess.

JOAN: What I wish in the whole hooky world?

HARRY: what's that?

JOAN: I wish my husband were here.

    Beat.

HARRY: I think I can arrange that.

JOAN: Would you?

HARRY: Sure. Poof. Hi.

JOAN: ah. there you are.

    They kiss.

    Lights.

BEANE's apartment.

BEANE and MOLLY. The standing lamp is lit.

Pause.

MOLLY: hey Beane?

BEANE: yeah?

MOLLY: will you tell me a story?

BEANE: sure.

MOLLY: How about something that starts out Gloomy and ends Happy.

BEANE: How about the story of the night we met?

MOLLY: Oh good.

   MOLLY situates herself.

BEANE: The Night We Met. [Feel free to chime in at any time.]

MOLLY: [I'll help out where I can.]

BEANE: [Now this is before we know each other.]

MOLLY: [So I'm miserable.]

BEANE: [That's the least of your problems.]

MOLLY: [I am Inconsolable.]

BEANE: [You're Tortured and Oppressed.]

MOLLY: (*Off, as if to her oppressors.*) Get *Off* Me you Bastards, Leave Me To *Die*!

BEANE: [Exactly right.] OK: The Night We Met: (*Beat.*) It's Night.

MOLLY: I love this so far.

BEANE: and it's Dark.

The standing lamp dims, on cue.

MOLLY: This must be the gloomy part.

BEANE: It's Pitch Black. It's Super-black, you can't tell if your eyes are open.

MOLLY: It's very dark.

BEANE: And the power's out.

MOLLY: You're kidding.

BEANE: The power's *been* out.

MOLLY: The *Bastards.*

BEANE: and the power's *staying* out.

MOLLY: Where'd I put that flashlight?

BEANE: and as Black as it is, as Deep Dark as it is, that's *nothing* compared to how Hot it is.

MOLLY: It's *hot?*

BEANE: Fry an egg on the sidewalk.

MOLLY: It's a *Scorcher.*

BEANE: Fry an egg on an Ice cube.

MOLLY: It's a *Sizzler.*

BEANE: So hot you can *hear* the heat.

MOLLY: (*To the heat, as it were.*) Shut up!

BEANE: The heat *fills* your mind with the droning sound of Hot.

MOLLY: SHUT UP!

BEANE: But it won't.

MOLLY: I'm *miserable.*

BEANE: You lie in your bed.

MOLLY: and I *sweat.*

BEANE: Your breath burns your throat.

MOLLY: I am Inconsolable.

BEANE: The sweat pools on your sheets.

MOLLY: I'm blistering, baking, boil water in my mouth.

BEANE: You feel your flesh cooking.

MOLLY: I feel my soul *evaporating.*

BEANE: And you lie there in the lightless dark and the super-hot heat and you Suffer.

MOLLY: fuck.

BEANE: and all the way uptown, in my own lightless hovel, I do too.

MOLLY: You're oppressed?

BEANE: I am tortured.

MOLLY: Are you hot?

BEANE: I'm *singed.*

MOLLY: We're *Miserable.*

BEANE: We lie there and we moan and we wallow and suffer.

MOLLY: We Realize that we have to get up.

BEANE: before the droning heat burns our brains to a crisp.

MOLLY: I gotta get outta here.

BEANE: So you stumble from your bed.

MOLLY: It's dark, Jesus.

BEANE: You grope your way to the door.

MOLLY: I'd light a match, but it's too fucking *hot.*

BEANE: You feel your way down the stairs.

MOLLY: out the door to the street.

BEANE: Where it's Soup.

MOLLY: Where it's Lava.

BEANE: Where it's Quiet.

Pause. Quiet.

MOLLY: (*Whispering.*) Where is everyone?

BEANE: They're at home.

MOLLY: They're in bed.

BEANE: They lie in the super-black. Their brains are burning.

MOLLY: I'm all alone out here.

BEANE: Me too.

MOLLY: I stumble down the street.

BEANE: into a pole.

MOLLY: ow.

BEANE: a parked car.

MOLLY: my *knee.*

BEANE: a Brick Wall of Heat.

MOLLY: *Ow*, Christ, it's Fucking *Dark.*

BEANE: You're stuck inside a mitten.

MOLLY: I Can't *See*!

BEANE: You're a muffled infant, in a boiling womb.

MOLLY: I fall to my knees.

BEANE: You crawl your way across the melting pavement.

MOLLY: over sidewalk and curb, over asphalt and pothole.

BEANE: over litter and vomit.

MOLLY: over *dis*carded gum.

BEANE: over filth and disease.

MOLLY: through a puddle of death.

BEANE: onto grass.

MOLLY: onto grass?

BEANE: You crawl into the park.

    Beat.

MOLLY: You come in from the North, on raspberried knees.

BEANE: You come in from the South, bleeding from your palms.

MOLLY: The park is a Sewer.

BEANE: A steaming dump.

MOLLY: An aftermath.

BEANE: The grass is dead and stiff, a carpet of needles and rigor mortis.

MOLLY: I crawl across the carcass of a squirrel.

BEANE: His dry bones splinter and pierce your skin.

MOLLY: I crawl through a valley of syringes.

BEANE: The heat on your back like an iron saddle.

MOLLY: The droning heat in my mind like the world's loudest dial tone.

BEANE: You crawl across the park.

MOLLY: My belly drags on the ground.

BEANE: You slither down a rocky slope.

MOLLY: I slide down a muddy bank.

BEANE: To the edge of the water.

Beat.

MOLLY: I'm at the reservoir.

BEANE: I stand at the lip, I peel the shirt off my back.

MOLLY: I kick off my shoes.

BEANE: I peel my pants off my ass.

MOLLY: My sweat-soaked panties fall, a soggy thud when they hit the ground.

BEANE: I'm naked.

MOLLY: I am nude. I dive in.

BEANE: I hear a Sound.

MOLLY: I dive deep.

BEANE: I hear a Splash.

MOLLY: I dive down and deep and deep and down.

BEANE: I dive into the drink.

MOLLY: But I can't feel the water.

BEANE: It's not hot, it's not cold.

MOLLY: It's my temperature exactly.

BEANE: the same as my skin, the same as my blood.

MOLLY: You swim down through water that you can't feel.

BEANE: You do breaststroke through the senselessness.

MOLLY: You swim through the dark, you are blind, dumb and numb.

BEANE: through the sameness.

MOLLY: the nothing.

BEANE: the same nothing.

MOLLY: the nothing.

BEANE: You come up from the deep for air that holds no promise, for air that will choke, for thick toxic hot –

MOLLY: I see you.

The standing light brightens to brilliance. The room is flooded with clearness. Pause.

BEANE: And your eyes gleam in the pitch. and your hair reflects the light that doesn't shine.

MOLLY: And in the deafness of the buzzing heat I hear you breathe.

BEANE: And through the senseless water I feel a ripple from your beating heart.

Pause.

MOLLY: hi.

BEANE: hi.

MOLLY: fancy meeting you here.

Pause.

BEANE: and a breeze blows.

MOLLY: Aren't you the guy with the cup?

BEANE: a cool breeze ripples the water.

MOLLY: I've been looking for you.

BEANE: a little breeze, as God looks at us and sighs.

MOLLY: I've been wanting to do something.

BEANE: a star shines.

MOLLY: I swim closer.

BEANE: a single star gets up from his sweaty bed and goes back to work.

MOLLY: I kiss you. (*She doesn't.*)

Pause.

BEANE: holy mackerel.

MOLLY: I swim closer.

BEANE: I don't know if the water just got colder or if my blood is boiling.

MOLLY: I rest my hand on the back of your neck.

BEANE: I rise to the top. I am shockingly buoyant.

MOLLY: I wrap my legs around your waist.

BEANE: Will you kiss me again?

MOLLY: Sure.

BEANE: Will you climb into my mouth?

MOLLY: I will live among your teeth, I'll build a house on your molars.

BEANE: Do you mind if I swallow you?

MOLLY: Not at all.

BEANE: I feel you slide down my throat.

MOLLY: It's warm.

BEANE: and into my belly.

MOLLY: slosh slosh.

BEANE: I digest you.

MOLLY: I'm nourishing.

BEANE: and delicious.

MOLLY: You sweat me out through every pore.

BEANE: I piss you and shit you.

MOLLY: Surprisingly, I don't find this disgusting.

BEANE: And then I confess that every time I blink, I mourn the quarter-second I'm not staring into your eyes.

MOLLY: and I realize that I'll never sleep again.

BEANE: and when I say your Name, I curse the smallness of speech, The audacious 'M' and 'O,' the two lousy 'L's and pathetic 'Y' that would fain Represent you.

MOLLY: I'll never eat unless you feed me.

BEANE: And when I touch the least of you, a wrinkled elbow, a callused heel, the very least of you makes me screech and purr and howl.

MOLLY: I'll never drink but from your mouth.

BEANE: And when I think of you I lose the scratching static in my head, I lose the nagging buzz that drowns me, Every time I think of you: I lose my mind.

A knock on the door. Three quick raps.

Pause. MOLLY and BEANE freeze, as if caught. Pause.

Another knock. Three quick raps.

MOLLY: (*To BEANE, sotto.*) Who's that?

Pause. BEANE is silent.

(*Sotto.*) Beane, who *is* that?

JOAN: (*From off.*) Beane.

BEANE: it's my sister.

Another knock. Five raps.

MOLLY: (*Sotto.*) We'll hide.

BEANE: Molly.

MOLLY: Keep *quiet.*

BEANE: She has a key.

JOAN: (*From off.*) Beane it's me!

MOLLY: (*Yelling off.*) Go Away!

> *Another knock. Five raps.*

> (*Yelling off.*) GO AWAY!

BEANE: Molly.

JOAN: (*From off.*) Come on open up!

MOLLY: (*Yelling off.*) I SAID GO AWAY!

JOAN: (*From off.*) Beane!

MOLLY: [Jesus Christ what is *wrong* with this woman] GO
AWAY. LEAVE US ALONE!

BEANE: Molly she can't hear you.

> *Pause. MOLLY looks at BEANE. BEANE looks at MOLLY then
> at the floor.*

> *Then the sound of keys inserted into the lock. Keys turning.*

> *MOLLY crosses to the bathroom. She closes the door behind her,
> simultaneously, the front door opens and the lights dim. BEANE
> sits alone in the near-dark. JOAN and HARRY enter. HARRY
> carries a bottle of champagne and four glasses.*

> *Pause.*

JOAN: (*With a recognition of something amiss.*) …surprise.

> *Pause.*

> *Lights.*

SCENE NINE

JOAN and HARRY's apartment.

Later that evening.

JOAN: We heard them *talking*.

HARRY: We heard *him* talking.

JOAN: Don't start with the Parsing, Harry, and the fucking Nitpicking and your precious Logic, You will find a way to dis*agree* with me and you will call it Irrefutable and Self-Evident, You know what it is? It's dis*agree*able.

HARRY: Say she was in the room.

JOAN: That *is* what I'm saying.

HARRY: Say you heard her talking.

JOAN: and I'm not *saying* that Harry, That is what *happened*, it's not a *position*.

HARRY: Right.

JOAN: I *heard* them.

HARRY: You heard them talking.

JOAN: *Yes*.

HARRY: Right. So first you hear them through the door, then what, then we walk in.

JOAN: I was *there*, Harry, I don't need a recap.

HARRY: We walk in: [and here's where it gets interesting] 'Cause we *Enter*. and she's not there.

Beat.

JOAN: What's your point.

HARRY: My point is she's not there.

JOAN: What kind of point is that? I *saw* that, I *recognize* that.

HARRY: My point is Where did she *go*?

JOAN: She went to the bathroom.

HARRY: The bathroom.

Pause.

JOAN: What.

HARRY: She slipped into the bathroom.

JOAN: Maybe she hates us.

HARRY: She's never *seen* us.

JOAN: She's a *Fanatic*, Harry, she's an *Extremist*, she hates the *sound* of us.

HARRY: Right. So she hears us coming, she slips into the bathroom.

JOAN: I would hate us too, if I were her, I would *despise* us, we're incredibly Boring.

HARRY: Right. So then what: We're in the apartment. We sit with Beane in silence for six hours, Then what happens.

JOAN: Can we not do the blow-by-every-fucking-miniscule-*blow* of this thing?

HARRY: You *insist* that you have to pee.

JOAN: What's that mean? I had to pee.

HARRY: Of course.

JOAN: I had to pee.

HARRY: But when you go in, –

JOAN: I HAD TO PEE.

HARRY: Right. But when you go *in*, [over Beane's sort of whimpered objections,] when you go into the *bath*room: She's not there.

Pause.

Jo. She's not in the bathroom.

JOAN: She's a burglar.

HARRY: How is that relevant.

JOAN: She slipped out. She shimmied down a drainpipe, or whatever it is they do. She's an expert.

Pause.

HARRY: Jo.

JOAN: What.

HARRY: There's no window.

Pause.

She expertly shimmied down a drainpipe because she hates us and who wouldn't, Except for there's no window in that bathroom and you know there isn't because you were just in there.

Pause.

JOAN: What's your point.

HARRY: My *Point?*

JOAN: I'm not sure what you're tiresomely driving at.

HARRY: What do you think *Happened?*

JOAN: She left.

HARRY: She crawled down the *drain?*

JOAN: Who can say.

HARRY: *Anyone* can say, any *sane* person can say with *Assurance* that she didn't crawl down the *drain.*

JOAN: That's your theory, Harry, I never said she crawled down the drain.

HARRY: There's no *Window*.

JOAN: We've established that.

HARRY: So what do you think *Happened*?

JOAN: I don't *know*.

HARRY: What *conceivably*, do you have a *notion*, what do you *think may* have happened?

JOAN: I said I don't *know*.

HARRY: Do you have a *theory*?

JOAN: I don't CARE.

HARRY: Do you care if your brother is insane?

JOAN slaps him, hard across the face. Pause.

I have a theory.

JOAN: (*Re: the slap.*) [I'm sorry.]

HARRY: You have a woman. Let's say she has no last name and an incredibly unlikely profession.

JOAN: [Harry please stop talking.]

HARRY: [I'm not finished.]

JOAN: [I'm asking nicely.]

HARRY: (*Lifting a coaster from the table. Evenly.*) [If you hit me again I'm going to fight back.]

Beat.

JOAN: [That's a coaster.]

HARRY: [I don't care what it is.]

Pause. HARRY holds the coaster between them.

And let's say this woman, Why don't we say that no one's ever *seen* her.

JOAN: I'm getting a glass of wine.

HARRY: But one day, Once Upon a *Time*, why don't we say, The Woman *Appears* in the Night.

JOAN: What if I put the robe on? Will you stop if I put on the robe?

HARRY: She *Rides* in, glass slippers, She Sees Beane [who, how should we describe Beane, let's just say he's not exactly *eligible* –]

JOAN: Please? Does it help if I say please?

HARRY: He's *compromised*, why don't we say.

JOAN: Harry?

HARRY: But the Thief finds him *Mesmerizing*! She finds him *Captivating*!

JOAN: I don't want to talk about it, ok?

HARRY: They fall Head over Heels, He is Trans*formed*! He is Saved! Hallelujah!

JOAN: I'm going to bed.

HARRY: Which would be great, God bless him, we should all be so lucky, Except for one thing.

JOAN: Goodnight Harry I'm sorry I hit you.

HARRY: She's not real.

Pause. JOAN does not leave.

She's terrific, Jo, Everyone adores her, she *lights* up a room, except she doesn't exist.

Pause.

JOAN: yeah well so what.

Pause.

HARRY: Sorry, excuse me, 'so what'?

JOAN: so what.

HARRY: She's not *Real*!

JOAN: People have different strengths.

HARRY: Are you *Joking*?

JOAN: Not really.

HARRY: Do you [Hold on] Do you *Recognize* that's he's [I don't even know what you *call* it] '*Dating*' someone who isn't a *person*?

JOAN: yes, alright?

HARRY: and that this is a *clear* sign that something is very *Wrong* with him.

JOAN: There's nothing wrong with him.

HARRY: He's *Hallucinating*.

JOAN: He's daydreaming.

HARRY: Except [that's fine, you're right, he is] except that he *thinks* she *exists*, it's great except that he *Believes* in her.

JOAN: does he?

HARRY: Doesn't he?

JOAN: I don't know.

HARRY: He thinks they've had *relations*.

JOAN: Oh, Harry, if you go by that, I've had sex with every moron in my office.

HARRY: No, it's Monu*mentally* – You may think *about* having sex with every moron, but you don't actually think you *have had sex* with every moron.

JOAN: So it's a difference of degree.

HARRY: Excuse me? She's Made *Up*! When she drinks *water* from a glass, the glass stays *full*. It's the same amount of water no matter how much she drinks, she can drink the fucking water all *day* and the glass never *moves*, because there's no one *there*!

JOAN: I understand your point, Harry.

HARRY: I don't think you *do*. My point is your brother thinks she's *real*. My point is he's in a full-blown Romance with *Nothing*, my point is this makes him *crazy*.

JOAN: it makes him happy.

Pause.

HARRY: I…excuse me but I don't think that's *responsible*.

Beat.

JOAN: (*A melancholy little laugh.*) hah.

HARRY: You're *related* to the guy.

JOAN: I am. [You're funny.] (*Beat.*) You're right, Harry. He's a nut-job. He's out of his mind. He always has been, every day of his shitty life. Then he was happy for a little while. For a week, he was happy. I'm glad he was, ok? I liked him better when she was around.

Beat.

HARRY: Jo, –

JOAN: And I liked us better too.

Lights.

SCENE TEN

BEANE's apartment.

Darkness.

BEANE crosses to the standing lamp. He turns it on. Dim light.

BEANE observes the lamp. He wears his overcoat.

The light dims. And then the walls converge.

BEANE is not resigned, he does not sigh. BEANE shakes the lamp by its throat, trying to wrest more light. The light dims further.

He then crosses to a wall and leans against it, resisting.

He pushes hard, his feet slip. He stumbles, he rights himself, he pushes against the wall.

The walls continue to converge, slowly, inexorably, inward.

BEANE fights.

Lights.

SCENE ELEVEN

BEANE's apartment.

BEANE sits at the table. JOAN knocks as she enters through the unlocked door. She stands just inside.

Pause. BEANE does not look at her, but he knows she's there.

BEANE: will you do me a favor?

JOAN: Sure.

Beat.

BEANE: will you touch my head?

JOAN crosses to BEANE. She stands behind him. With an outstretched arm, she places her palm on top of his head. Pause.

JOAN: How's that.

BEANE: It's ok.

Pause.

JOAN: How're you doing.

Pause.

Did you eat today?

BEANE: Is it Thursday?

JOAN: you know I'm not sure.

BEANE: I ate on Thursday.

Pause.

JOAN: Are you hungry?

BEANE: No.

JOAN: I could order you something.

BEANE: that's ok.

Pause.

JOAN: (*Re: the hand on head.*) Should I keep doing this?

BEANE: please.

Pause.

It's multi-purpose.

JOAN: I see.

Pause.

BEANE: There's no window in the bathroom.

JOAN: I know.

Pause.

BEANE: I'm not sure what they expect from you. I'm supposed to live among the various Smells, I guess. They don't let you air the fucking bathroom out, I'm not sure that's so much to ask.

JOAN: I'm sorry Beane.

BEANE: It's inconvenient.

JOAN: I know it is.

BEANE: Isn't glass made from sand?

JOAN: Something like that.

BEANE: Sand is free.

Pause.

It seems like they're out to get you, after a while it's not only that they're cheap, it's that they're Mean.

Pause.

Do you want a glass of wine?

JOAN: I'm fine.

BEANE: I know how you like a glass of wine sometimes.

JOAN: I'm ok.

BEANE: I sort of want to poke my eyes out.

JOAN: Don't do that.

Pause.

(*Re: her arm which she removes from BEANE's head.*) Can I take this off? I'm getting a cramp.

BEANE: you bring a marching band stomping through your heart and all of a sudden you can smell cookies baking halfway across the city. Now I can't switch it off. I have to smell the full awful when there's no window in the bathroom.

Pause.

JOAN: Can I sit?

BEANE: (*Resting his head on the tabletop.*) I'm just gonna rest this thing a minute.

JOAN: (*Sitting at the table with BEANE.*) Remember Tim Adair?

Pause.

Beane?

BEANE: I remember he broke your heart that time and you wouldn't come out of your room. That was when Mom couldn't hear you unless you held her by the ears and screamed into her face.

JOAN: I wrote his book reports.

BEANE: (*Lifting his head from the table.*) why?

JOAN: because I loved him more than life itself.

BEANE: I guess that's a good reason.

JOAN: Then he left me for that new girl with the jeans.

BEANE: What's-her-face.

JOAN: That night, I was up in my room. [You remember this?]
It was dinner time and Mom kept calling,

BEANE: 'Dinner, hoo-hoo, Dinner.' *

JOAN: [Yeah, God, 'hoo-hoo'] and I was sitting on the edge of
the bed, and I was Crying. (*Beat.*) Just heaving, you know,
the end of the world, Snot. [you know that thing,] You're
crying so hard you can't make space between the sobs
to Breathe. (*Beat.*) I was touching myself. for comfort, I
dunno, I had my hands down my pants. (*Beat.*) He had that
yellow bicycle.

BEANE: yeah.

JOAN: and so there I am keening, and masturbating, I'm
sloshing around in six kinds of fluid…and I can remember
Seeing myself. Observing myself from above, looking
down at this *puddle.* (*Beat.*) I remember thinking, very
distinctly I remember thinking: Look at that. Look at her.
How I've been Rendered by this boy. This shallow boy,
this Paper Bag has Obliterated me, *look* at that. (*Beat.*) and
I said, 'This is the last time,' out loud, I actually swore to
myself, The Last Time that I will be made a *Fool* of by
Feelings. (*Beat.*) I zipped up my pants and wiped my face
on the sheets and I started my life.

Pause.

I jumped my husband yesterday.

Pause.

I kissed his feet and made him scream like a baboon and I
cried on his shoulder and lay there next to him and traced
pictures on his stomach with my finger.

BEANE: …Jo.

---

* *A sing-song imitation of their mother.*

89

JOAN: because of you.

BEANE: She's not real.

JOAN: I don't care.

BEANE: She's not Real.

JOAN: I don't care who she is, Beane. I saw what she was to you. I don't think it matters.

BEANE: it matters if you're me.

Pause.

am I ok?

JOAN: Of course you are.

BEANE: are you sure?

JOAN: You're a little lonely.

Pause.

You want a cigarette?

BEANE: ok.

JOAN lights BEANE an imaginary cigarette, she hands it to him. She lights one for herself.

I didn't know you smoked.

JOAN: I just took it up.

They smoke. Pause.

BEANE: This is delicious.

Beat.

I want to hide.

JOAN: You can if you like.

BEANE: I want to hide in my room and never be found. I want to sit very still and eventually I turn to ash and in a hundred years I get swept up by a guy with a dustpan.

JOAN: Well I'm afraid that's not an option.

BEANE: why not?

JOAN: You have a sister.

Pause.

I'll tell you what.

JOAN knocks three times on the table top. She then looks at the door as if the knock has come from outside.

Who could that be?

BEANE: what.

JOAN: There's someone at the door.

BEANE: oh, Joey, come on.

JOAN knocks again on the table.

JOAN: (*Shouting off.*) One Second! (*Then to BEANE.*) I'm gonna go. Give you two some privacy.

BEANE: Jo, you can't just – That's not how it works.

JOAN: Really? How does it work?

Beat. BEANE has no answer.

(*Rising, crossing to the door.*) I'll call you tomorrow. You figure out what you want. I'm gonna go home and fuck my husband.

JOAN exits. BEANE is at the wooden table. Pause. Pause.

BEANE: oh what the hell.

The bathroom door opens. MOLLY enters.

MOLLY: (*Sniffing the air.*) Smells like smoke.

BEANE: very funny.

MOLLY: (*Holding up a bottle of whiskey.*) I brought you a present.

BEANE: Is it real?

Beat.

MOLLY: Is this how this is gonna be now?

BEANE: I'm just curious.

MOLLY opens the bottle, holds it upside down. Nothing comes out.

MOLLY: Does that answer your question?

BEANE: saves on cleanup, I guess.

MOLLY pulls BEANE's cup from her pocket. She pours. The whiskey fills the cup without any obvious adjustment to the bottle. MOLLY hands the full cup to BEANE.

MOLLY: (*A toast.*) Death to Literalism.

MOLLY drinks from the bottle. BEANE drinks from the cup. Beat.

BEANE: You know there's a theory going around.

MOLLY: People will talk.

BEANE: They're saying I made you up.

MOLLY: Is that right?

BEANE: That I created you. You're a figment of my imagination.

MOLLY: Is that what they're saying?

BEANE: yeah.

MOLLY: What do *you* think?

BEANE: I think they have it backwards.

MOLLY: How do you mean.

BEANE: I think you created *me*.

Pause.

I used to be flat and quiet. I was wallpaper. I stayed very still. I met you and I became real. I ate and drank, I left footprints. I had Volume. When I entered a room there were more people there.

Beat.

MOLLY: You know I could say the same.

BEANE: You? Please. You're fearsome.

MOLLY: I was a Scab. I was a burned and crusty Lizard that lay on a wound. You dissolved me. I got melted. Now I have a squishy middle. I'm a jelly donut.

Beat.

BEANE: Molly.

MOLLY: yeah.

BEANE: I've been Alive in my life for a single week.

MOLLY: A lifetime of waiting.

BEANE: of pacing the platform.

MOLLY: Years of starvation.

BEANE: and then a Week-Long Feast.

MOLLY: A week in the Light.

BEANE: A week in the Wow.

MOLLY: When all of a sudden, the love songs make sense.

BEANE: They'd been sung all my life in Greek and Pig-Latin.

MOLLY: They were Gibberish.

BEANE: Rubbish.

MOLLY: Hostile nonsense.

BEANE: making fun behind my back.

MOLLY: Then for a week: I know all the words.

BEANE: The songs ring out from every speaker.

MOLLY: They sing to me in my Mother Tongue.

BEANE: I've always known that life was meant for other people. that air and sun and conversation, I wasn't born to these things. You brought matches and desire and you set fire to my soggy self. Now I'm alive. I have the courage to want. I wanna make speeches from the balcony and buy hotdogs from vendors. I wanna piss off the roof and play catch with an egg.

Pause.

MOLLY: you want to go outside.

BEANE: You made me brave.

MOLLY: You want to go outside.

Pause.

I have certain strengths, Beane. I'm not so good at the outside part.

Pause.

BEANE: Molly.

MOLLY: Listen: I'm not a person who asks a lot of favors.

BEANE: I'm sorry.

MOLLY: I am known for my self-reliance. I don't plead.

BEANE: I think I have to try it.

MOLLY: I'm gonna make an exception: please. don't leave me.

Pause.

Beane. please don't make me go.

Pause. Then MOLLY slowly lifts her hands above her head.

(An offering.) I surrender.

Pause.

BEANE: I'm sorry.

Beat. Then MOLLY slowly lowers her hands to her sides.

MOLLY: I see.

Pause.

BEANE: I think I have to try the thing of people.

MOLLY: ok.

BEANE: I have to try.

MOLLY: I understand.

BEANE: don't I?

MOLLY: it does seem like the brave thing.

Pause.

BEANE: Molly.

MOLLY: No, come on. You're not the only wack-job in the ocean.

BEANE: I'm so sorry.

MOLLY: Don't be. Couple of weeks drunk, I'm as good as new.

Beat. MOLLY crosses to BEANE, kisses him full on the mouth. A deep, sexy, passionate, big-time kiss.

Go find the flesh and blood, Beane. Make me proud.

MOLLY crosses to the door.

MOLLY: I'm keeping the outfit.

BEANE: I think that's fair.

MOLLY is at the door.

BEANE: Molly.

Beat. MOLLY stops.

I don't know who I am without you.

MOLLY: you'll be fine.

BEANE: I don't know if that's true.

MOLLY: take a walk. eat something, read the paper. try a little life. if you hate it, you know where to find me.

Beat.

BEANE: I don't want to be dead again.

MOLLY: so don't be. Live.

MOLLY exits through the front door. Pause. BEANE crosses to the lamp. He touches the lamp. It brightens to brilliance.

The End.